specimens

Mark Cunningham

Also by Mark Cunningham

Books

71 Leaves. Ebook. BlazeVOX. (2008). <www.blazevox.org/ebk-
       Cunningham%20REAL.pdf>.
Body Language. Tarpaulin Sky Press. (2008).
80 Beetles. Otoliths. (2008).

Chapbooks

Leftovers. Gold Wake Press. (2010).
       <www.goldwakepress.files.wordpress.com/2010/05/leftovers.pdf>.
Georgic, with Eclogues for Interrogators. Lamination Colony. (2009).
       <www.laminationcolony.com/GEORGICS/georgics.pdf>.
Color Field. (2009). 2River View.
       <www.2river.org/chapbooks/cunningham/pdf/cunningham.pdf>.
Nacträglichkeit. (2009). Beard of Bees. <www.beardofbees.com/pubs/Nachtraglichkeit.pdf>.
10 specimens. (2009). Gold Wake Press.
       <www.goldwakepress.files.wordpress.com/2009/08/tenspecimens.pdf>.
nightlightnight. (2009). Right Hand Pointing.
       <www.righthandpointing.com/nightlightnight>.
Second Story. (2006). Right Hand Pointing.
       <www.righthandpointing.com/markcunningham/cunningham.pdf>.
Body. Mudlark Poster 43 (2002). <www.unf.edu/mudlark/posters/cunningham.html>.

specimens

Mark Cunningham

BlazeVOX [books]

Buffalo, New York

Specimens by Mark Cunningham
Copyright © 2011

Published by BlazeVOX [books]

All rights reserved. No part of this book may be reproduced without
the publisher's written permission, except for brief quotations in reviews.

Printed in the United States of America
Book design by Geoffrey Gatza

First Edition
ISBN: 978-1-60964-054-5
Library of Congress Control Number 2010943105

BlazeVOX [books]
303 Bedford Ave
Buffalo, NY 14216

Editor@blazevox.org

publisher of weird little books

BlazeVOX [books]

blazevox.org

BlazeVOX

Thanks to Emily Howard and Linda Kobert.

Parts of this book, sometimes in different form, have appeared in *The American Drivel Review, BlazeVOX, Cannot Exist, Clockwise Cat, Counterexample Poetics, Denver Quarterly, diode, Eoagh, e:ratio, Everyday Genius, Fact-Simile, Great Works, kill author, Laura Hird, Otoliths, Parcel, Sawbuck, Spine Road, Tarpaulin Sky, Unlikely Stories*, and the chapbooks *10 Specimens* and *Leftovers*, both published by Gold Wake Press.

specimens

10 specimens

We watched Micrea Cantor's *Deeparture*, in which a deer and a wolf lie, stand, or pace in a white-walled room, too bored to flee or hunt, then we looked at the other exhibits in the gallery. To be a sentence is to be in line. No spam for four days means something is wrong.

I *am* being objective: the object vanished at the vanishing point. It was all boarded up, so we couldn't tell what it was. Turns out it was a bunch of boards nailed together. He kept saying, "Main point? There is no main point," but I'm pretty sure he was throwing his voice.

He always spoke of elsewhere and, in fact, his breath always ended up in a different place. In the interest of transparency, the Board of Directors made itself invisible. Virginia Woolf complained of "this appalling narrative business of the realist: getting on from lunch to dinner, it is false, unreal, merely conventional," and, in fact, every day thousands do not make it. The objects drew attention to themselves by costing money.

"He means nothing to me. He's just a friend." I wasn't chatting her up: I was discoursing. I shared a quote laugh unquote with him. A second look showed me the notice did not read "remaindered larynxes."

The music of the spheres is an air leak, as you can tell when you say "spheres," but knowing this only makes me whistle to myself more when I'm scared at night. I was docked points because I couldn't remember who wrote the book on the death of the author. The tribe's ideal height was two feet, so the archeologist figured the graves would be two feet deep. That she was cutting herself was one thing; what was really creepy was that they were all paper cuts.

He said, "We're all partly violent monsters in our subconscious minds and that's why we have laws," and I said, "Let go of me." The line was flat as could be, but to call it "deadpan" seemed life-denying. He made a funny face and hurt himself. When the doctor brought out the anatomically-incorrect doll, my fingernails started to sweat even more. Weinermobile Wrecks Home.

We couldn't figure out how to be sure time was accurate. The buffet offered chicken from The Dutch Golden Age. Did enough happen to keep a sit-com going: that's how we judge our lives.

Once we figured out it wasn't a real head but a log woodpeckers had gouged into the human semblance, we were able to explain a few things. We knew it was her style because it was so impersonal. "Nothing's happening." "That's one thing." You could see the metal shed was there because the glare made it impossible to look in that direction.

He wanted to show me the line "all sleep may be a mood," but since he woke me up to show me, I was in no mood to look. I used to talk to myself, but I always said the wrong thing. I told a joke, but it turns out the committee had a gag reflex. Those stars are the heroes who've gone before us with *their* cigarette lighters. The scientists thanked us for our input but said *they* would decide what "objective" is.

When I discovered my natural self, I realized the new medication had worked. From the ridge, we had an unobstructed view of the light pollution. As we drove through downtown, he said, "This must be what downtown looked like thirty years ago." He turned the page to continue his essay on why motion is impossible.

75 specimens

I'm never the person I remember being. The eyelids sense things the eyes can't see. What I thought was someone moving in a window was me blinking. "Present being" is incapable of being presented and an order.

Believers in the Flood, heads up: in Corot's *Eel Gatherers*, one of the boys is half-way up a tree. Where are you? Right here. I know *that*. The night smelled very clean: I can't remember ever having been so afraid.

The video of the starlings swirling and swarming and eddying was wall-sized: I kept looking at an unused wall socket to keep my balance. Squinting through the bay-shimmer, the girl pointed and, in a lull between waves, called out, "There's some trash!"

He started to wander inwardly, but he didn't get very far due to clogged arteries. That history decays into images and not into stories is the only thing Walter Benjamin wrote that I can remember. I couldn't understand the words she was whispering, but the foam sticking to my ear spoke loud and clear.

Pornography is an aid to memory. The problem with trauma is that you really never are alone. The first viewers of the Lumiere Brother's films were captivated not by the people moving—they'd seen zoetropes and kinetoscopes—but by the plants shifting. "Fucking brilliant" doesn't usually refer to the body.

The moon and my bar of soap show the scars of various impacts. Lacan points out that you can detect the presence of the unconscious mind in the interruptions and blanks in conscious thought or speech. We stepped on the black mat and the door didn't swing open, so we just pushed it and went in. No entrance can be dead.

There's the idea of a tree in my head, but in the reflection of my head there's a real tree. I was supposed to read out loud Artaud's sentence, "What voluntary breathing brings about is a spontaneous reappearance of life," but I got on stage, took a deep breath, and forgot my line. The appendix is a numb tongue. The tongue is a fine ear: shut your mouth and you can't hear as well.

She told me she'd make me eat my words, so I started saying her name over and over.
She ate something that disagreed with her. Rape (mustard).

Each person needs a special "mount yell." Anthropoltergeist. Was it uh-huh passive,
like *I'm listening*, or uh-huh active, as in *that is too the case*?

As I walked into the room, I told myself, *don't start throbbing now*. The Thai-English phrase book had nothing for *Will you try not to wobble*? Robins are not very good at acting casual. My favorite kind of green beans are those that start out purple and turn green as you boil them. Trees are circular, but even if I say *there's something behind that tree*, I still haven't pinpointed where *I* am.

Bodies absorb sound, so she used me as a human shield whenever the Proactiv commercials came on. He said he was going to the protest against Daylight Savings Time, but he stayed up too late and overslept. The history test was tough and my deodorant failed. As Darwin explained, "The expression of grief, due to a contraction of the grief muscles." I said I was really sad, and she said photographic evidence shows that no face is really straight.

I can't tell if the line fragment is clenching point A and point B closer together or if point A and point B are stretching the line fragment farther in both directions. I drank to fill the hole in my experience. Now I have a specific experience: a hole in my stomach.

A thimble holds a million trillion trillion trillion electrons at any moment and I can still get my thumb inside, but I've just had to go up another waist size. It was an important moment in evolution, so we filmed it and put the clip on the internet so people could watch it and laugh. Since when does "leatherette" not mean "female leather?" The ideogram for *the great learning* is *grinding the corn in the head's mortar to fit it for use*—but, ha, now our *whole body* is made of corn.

Enraged, the beetle made its video game noise. The superhero stunned us all with his cat hiss. When I kept asking her to wear the long, lacy lingerie, she knew it was time for us to watch the Mexican horror movies again. The billiards table was inspired by the great Pacific Northwest. Of course I knew it was you: I'd recognize that Marlene Dietrich impersonation anywhere.

She said she'd been touched by my emotions, and I wondered *how am I going to show this using the doll?* He said the deer came out of nowhere, and then he pointed to the spot. Easy for you to say I'm an echo. I told him his repetition compulsion indicated childhood trauma, and he said read the instructions on the shampoo for yourself.

I'd be surprised if someone named Bear *hadn't* seen *Gremlins* at least five times. "That it is able to be returned to makes something's existence more probable." He said it wasn't a hair; it was a special spice. I had to agree with him. It was the best tasting hair I ever ate. My itchy ankles distracted me from my existential crisis. I read about it in this super-secret lost book of lost super-secrets that I bought at Barnes and Noble.

He started to explain how the particles pass in and out of existence too fast to be detected, but we didn't have time to listen to a lot of fourth-dimension nonsense. First Kentucky thought it was Southern, then North Carolina claimed to be tropical, then the Arctic Circle said it was the Antarctic Circle and, at some point, I couldn't tell the difference any more. The universe is expanding, but the latest calculations show it's still supported at its edges only by widely-spaced stacks of cinder blocks. We learned a lot from the section titled "Use of Lime Plaster to Integrate Profane and Symbolic Realms."

A sloping pattern of shine and shade is just as much a Rorschach as anything else, but most of us have learned that the correct answer is "hill." I got the first rock in my shoe while putting the shoe on.

Her piece on how she stopped thinking in terms of "meat" was well-done, which is rare for that medium. I saw Wolfgang Laib's *Without Place--Without Time--Without Body* in Kansas City at 3:43 on Thursday, and I liked the side view the best.

The clouds are not in the sky, they are in the air (the sky clouded over). I've seen the old woman in the puzzle, and that settles that. "To think is to converse, but (only) with oneself," but I always tilt my head, because I'm deaf in one ear. When Bob said he was a positivist, I felt a little push in the back, though there was no one standing behind me.

We couldn't remember if "reverse osmosis" meant we got stupider when we were asleep or when we woke up. The book had an entire chapter that offered us a variety of writing experiments to help us discover our own secrets. He kept going on about the American Dream, but he didn't even try to look at his hands.

The stewardess kept gesturing with her index and middle fingers, but only business class knew the proper gang response. Apparently, one of the rules of tai chi is that you have to practice in a busy public place. Who could a poster showing the remains of one of the World Trade Center towers with the caption "Steel Standing" appeal to, other than Hispanic marines? The man wearing a cowboy hat stood next to a bale of cardboard.

According to the military, the United States is supposed to be everywhere and visible; according to *National Geographic*, the United States is supposed to be everywhere and invisible. That time of day when to see through a window you walk straight toward your reflection. You need a mullet to know which way the wind blows.

The fifteen-year-old put down the phone and asked his brother wearing an I Can Wait t-shirt, "Did I sound professional enough?" I had a crush on a woman because she was a dead ringer for Leni Riefenstahl in *The Holy Mountain*. His special interest group's viewpoint was that the situation was universal. I couldn't tell if the argument was from a right-wing talk show or a rap CD.

The brochure pointed out that Paleolithic man enjoyed a barbecue. Even Harpo yawns at the end of his harp solo in *Animal Crackers*. It's a good thing I don't see the sun in my dreams; everybody knows that seeing the sun is bad for your eyes. The freshman health class syllabus no longer refers to the "scrotum," but to the "cul-de-sac of the testicles." If Gomer Pyle were around today, he'd be a wigger.

The doctor asked if I had unprotected contact, and I said no, I usually had a weapon. The announcement said the junior high students were to dress business casual for their graduation. At least Newtonian physics led to miniature golf; quantum mechanics has led to ketchup as a vegetable. It's real, which means it's affiliated.

The red shift applies particularly to drying blood. He was foreign, so we had to talk louder. "Erasing memory causes heat to flow into the environment." Each generation knows less of history than the one before it, and global warming continues to get worse. At first, a mountain is just a mountain; then a mountain is not just a mountain; then it is a tourist spot.

I can't decide whether the social system works to block clear thinking. I remember where I was when I heard that Elvis had died. Bears must be pissed off to have to live where they are called "barrs" all the time. Of course I blew my own horn; no one else was in the car.

The article featured photographs of the top-secret aircraft that had been at the root of flying saucer reports. The policeman told me to recite the alphabet backwards from Q to D, and I could, so I knew I was drunk. We need to tinker with the memory machine. The first thing the patient remembered was that he had amnesia. She asked if I was frightened of uncertainty, and I was too scared to admit I'd never thought about it. "Keep your face to the sunshine and you cannot see the shadow"—Helen Keller said that.

Thomas Kincaid is the new super-realist: his mountains, rainy streets, and windows glow as if X-rays, microwaves from cell phone towers, and electro-magnetic pulse have soaked in for good. The recording had "room ambiance," which meant that it was a poor recording.

His trip to see the mountain gorillas in the wild changed his life: he started to go to the zoo regularly. I scratched my armpits in three different ways, and they didn't even notice. She backed herself into the corner and began throwing conference food, but that didn't keep them at bay for long. Even after the waterboarding, the mole held firm and said he wasn't going to be badgered. I felt threatened by her waving to the giant chicken right in the middle of our argument.

A dozen or so people influence what everybody in the world thinks, and everybody in the world hates them: that's what I call low self-esteem. The mere idea of a "freestanding subject that sprays out meaning" makes me want to puke. I asked if they were controlling my thoughts and they said no, so I guess that's that. My second personality claims it's schizophrenic, but I think it's just a hypochondriac.

Over the course of a lifetime, people inhale at least eight spiders in their sleep. Every day after school, she would eat creamed peas and listen to *Led Zeppelin I*. More plastic in that one hit than Visa has dropped on all Hiroshima. Hold it: now *I* can't remember the last time someone touched me. At some point, it becomes just a mass of hair. What do you mean, *maybe* that was your *Creature from the Black Lagoon* noise?

Yes, I did say I'd be shit on by a 12-ton pterodactyl and, yes, I did live—barely—to regret my words. We drove the monster off with a stick, but John's nose hair remained relentless. The whole universe, and plaque has to get right between your teeth where it will cause gum decay. The void: never around when you want it. Despite the ad campaign, some people are starting to recover their memories of Taco Tico.

I don't know if I like it: the chemical burn is still eating through the roof of my mouth. Since we were taking in part of our environment and extracting nutrients and we were seeing a black hazed with green and red light/dust like the Hubble telescope showed from deepest space, we held that our refusing to open our eyes formed a coherent world view. Even she had to admit she didn't have enough information to tell whether her statement "information doesn't apply to this situation" was accurate. Our arguments over whether it was his reflection or mine were oddly similar.

We drew the animal with big chunks missing from its body to show the waves were washing it and it was happy. When she asked if I believed in content, I knew she was getting at something, but I couldn't tell what. Her dream house was a hundred yards from the interstate and with the white noise of the cars passing all the time she could never tell if she was awake or asleep. All the subtitle said was, "vocalizing continues." You may think you're a nihilist, but try to kill yourself by holding your breath.

"My only joy is the hope last night has given me of sleeping better." It's good to have a place where you can go and be local. We could approach the sea by all ways except *by sea*. Right now, somebody at a red light somewhere is opening his car door to spit. They said the film did not take place in real time, but we still got older while we watched.

By "the repulsive intrusion of an animal's bodily excrescences" he meant "fur." Emily Dickinson's punctuation—is perfect—for the title cards—of silent movie comedies. If you play in slow motion the video of people speaking in a foreign language, you can tell they are really cursing in English. The sign was arbitrary, or so we decided to call it.

Somebody put a Domino's out here in nowhere; now the area is even more nowhere. He said a pine tree could also be used as wood. It doesn't really get cold until the earth starts to move back toward the sun. I raised the cup to drink, but even before it reached my mouth I had to swallow. Darkness is always less total than itself, and I have the bruise on my shin to prove it.

The sky turned smooth gray and then snow started to erase the ground, too. I was stunned when the bank teller identified me: I'd wrapped my head in Saran Wrap, and I thought packaging changed everything. If he says "everything is just beginning" one more time, I'll drop a 16-ton weight on him. I think I've figured out how to work the image duplicator. I think I've figured out how to work the image duplicator.

The ambient CD of forest rainfall was indistinguishable from light static—make that *lite* static—but it was a soothing lite static. I like those granola bars that look like particle board, because they make me feel I'm at home anywhere. I tried to pay attention, to write down every bodily sensation for five minutes without stopping, but my notes turned out to be *my right hand moves to the right, my right hand moves to the right, back left, to the right.* . . . We saw a sparrow fly straight into a closed window, so we counted our walk as a nature hike.

His main democratic belief was that anyone, *anyone*, can tighten his own drive belt and avoid costly repair. "Don't believe everything you think"—I say anything real enough for William James is real enough for me. Dolphins love to be near humans, but their ultrasound releases *endorphins* in us, and you still think they're so smart?

Like trying to tell the flavor of a Tootsie Pop in the dark. When they said it would take more than half the plank to reach shore, I said it depends on which half. Didn't the words "improvisational comedy" make you suspicious?

She said I was laboring under a false consciousness, and I said I can't believe my ears. Photography is not a documentary art, because you have to hold the camera right up to your eyes, and your hands aren't supposed to be in the frame, so you can't be sure you're not dreaming. Night is more time than space, but I can never find my watch to tell how much more.

Originally, people believed Van Gogh killed himself while he painted *Wheatfield with Crows*; then Artaud claimed Van Gogh painted it *almost* "at the precise moment he rid himself of existence," but then he noted Van Gogh painted it two days before he shot himself; now scholars state Van Gogh painted the canvas twenty days before he died. She told me she had two words for my idea, "*bor ring.*" I wish this thing had a 48-hour battery: I'm looking at a long night.

I took the test to see if I could foretell the future, and I could hardly sleep the whole week I had to wait for the results. Coffee gives you the serenity to dream it and the energy to do it: I turned on the flashlight to check the star chart. She said nature was a "multi-media performance piece," meaning that nothing important was going on. They thought I was capable of the unexpected, but they were in for a surprise. His pupils pin-pointed, but we just considered that dotting the i.

According to the theory of relativity, time slows to an almost complete halt the nearer you are to an "experimental film." That's right, Barbara Bush said at her birthday party, but then Isaac Newton couldn't tie a cherry stem into a knot with his tongue. Maybe in the beginning was the word, but now there just isn't that much left to say about it. Squinting at the photograph of the mirror, she said, "Are we supposed to be seeing something here?"

The kind of audience that responds to "bucks" instead of "dollars." We honky-tonked the abortion clinic bomber. To alleviate hunger and depression, we planted apples in their eyes. It was so visceral it made us all sentimental.

She didn't want to sleep in the cell where they were testing the stoat's response to extreme audio stimuli, but the team leader said it would be wearing headphones. The manager assured me these were the most wholesome chickpeas he had. The committee thought its memos were too impersonal, so it started to use emoticons. His greatest personal triumph was thinking up the phrase "so-called subjectivity." If she hadn't woken me up from the rescue fantasy, I don't know what would have happened.

The plants were mutating at a rate of one new species every twelve hours, and our "I am rubber, you are glue" defense was starting to falter. I'm not tapping my fingers in time with the country music: the injection of spider cells is finally taking hold. Among our demands was a more precise definition of "inedible." Gesturing to the horizon, he asked if I saw any other person here on the steppe and seemed non-plussed when I said, "one."

We didn't clone the baby, we cloned its sleep, since that would be more profitable and would keep our financial backers in power. The can't-wish-for-unlimited-wishes proviso shows the genie is on management's side. You can lead a concept to its self-critique, but no matter how much you get it to drink, it still keeps some of its clothes on. Today is the first day of the novelization of the rest of your life.

She said we must not confuse an individual with his or her work, which his just what
we expected someone in her position to say. It was a stare-down match, tense:
everybody knew that in the blink of an eye, one of us could blink. He was told to write
"Human beings are not insensate photocopying machines" on the blackboard one
hundred times. I laughed at their threat to articulate my skeleton if I kept giving them
the silent treatment—in that pile of bones, they'd never figure out which were mine.
XXX is better than X, so I figured $0.00 was better than $0.

The regional manager seemed ruffled when he heard that the illegals could remember pain for more than twenty-six seconds. It was a mirror image, but we couldn't tell of what. That lemur was so life-like, it had to have been machine-made. They gave me the date and the coordinates, but my shirt still didn't match. We watched the porn: it does less psychic damage than the Weather Channel.

The doctor said the patient was a danger only to herself, and the patient said we are all one. It was a test of character, but fortunately the questions were all multiple guess. She agreed that the peas were *non-canny*, anyway. Every time I start to read Husserl's *Phenomenology of Internal Time Consciousness*, I remember *The Andy Griffith Show* is on. No point counting your McNuggets, because you can't be sure they ever really hatched.

You can't throw a piece of tape very far. Transformation is tacky. "Mobile" gives no sense of social direction; "mobile home" does. He went to the cafeteria before we did, and when he returned he was able to tell us about our future.

"No one paid attention, but I did." Evidence that the world is a complete system usually ignores many things. As Robbe-Grillet writes, "I am a studious little girl." *Universal small town American experience.* You could tell it was her style because it was so impersonal. Those aren't paper wads; they're my origami model of the solar system. None of us in the expedition knew if the dead ringers could actually hear each other.

I was writing a book titled *My Life*, but someone told me it had already been written. $1 + 0 = 2$, because the situation would make anyone feel self-conscious. She was the type of person to say "and" instead of "to": be sure *and* wear your new shoes.

I tied a string around my finger to remind myself I was a puppet. He emphasized several times that he was going to say this only once. Flagrantly ignoring the last hundred years of physics, the insurance company claimed my past was a pre-existing condition. Regret is always hypothetical. Usually, you can still answer the question, how numb is it?

If we make their lives boring enough, they will come to serve our interests. I'm easily sold on a good idea, and the first idea they sold me was that their idea was good. I'm afraid of being alone in wide open spaces; fortunately, there's a chain restaurant in any really large parking lot. I couldn't tell if it was my mind or just a trick of the light.

When I asked why his description of the banana did not point out the peel was yellow, he said, "Because you can *see* that." We were in a slowness race to see whether we would free ourselves or whether capitalism would implode for good. When I saw the booger had disappeared from the end of my finger, yet was not on the Kleenex, I hesitated to approach the cashier. Adjust this, adjust that: most scales can't weigh zero accurately. The doctor said I wasn't feeling *real* phantom limb pain.

Every moment really is new: today in the woods I startled a squirrel and when it bolted away I could hear a crinkling rustle like plastic wrap being undone hastily. When he told me I shouldn't allow myself to form the concept of a road, I realized I'd made a wrong turn. Man Pretending to Fall off Bridge Actually Falls Off. Time saved is brain saved.

They tried to tell us it was a question of narrative, but we'd heard that story before. The world is everything that's just in case. "Persistence of vision" is another term for "persistence of blindness." The room was dark as a coal mine, but I knew where the mirror was, and I didn't want to sit facing it. Fill in the blank: the universe reminds me of _______.

I'm a performance artist in my 34th year of performing *Things to Do Instead of Writing a Duet for Flute and Bulldozer*, yet when I mention this, people still hear it. It's one of nature's most beautiful sounds: the great outdoors. Sometimes a light bulb just makes a noise. Meat products shouldn't snap. We didn't consider the suggestion to scream until we'd deafened ourselves and could no longer hear the rustling to be very empowering. I look like I'm standing here doing nothing, but really I'm calling your name in my head, quietly.

He never tired of saying he was against language. As he passed us on the trail, the mountain biker said, "There's only one of me." It's pointless for me to talk about my sleep habits: they are too intimate for me to know. It would have been nice if the Berlin Wall had fallen when no one was around, because then it wouldn't have made any noise.

After the tornado sirens didn't go off, we decided to hold a virtual town hall meeting, especially since no one could find the town. All images are local, but this doesn't tell you what "local" is. I repeat, all images are local. They couldn't believe it: I looked just like my photograph. The bottle had been recycled, and the note inside didn't have anything original to say, either.

"Xenophobia, steak and chips, cuckold jokes, in short, what we call an ideology."
There can't be a revolutionary party without peer pressure. Futurism is now: you have
to double click fast. 34 Hospitalized After Co-Worker Sprays Perfume. I had my finger
on the pulse of life, which means the pulse wasn't in my finger.

I moved and the vulture clattered away. The bare trees across the field thinned to smoke in the late sunlight. Yet they were still there the next morning. Sometimes nature tries to speed things up when it thinks you're not looking. When the father asked his son, "Do you know what's inside the Pentagon?" the son replied, "2,511 clocks." I was looking into the neon of Dan Flavin's "monument to V. Tatlin" and seeing the dust on my glasses.

We ran the numbers again, but the equation still checked out: David Spade was invited by *the Chinese*. The commercial showed the white kids in color and the black kids in black and white. So you *never* remember an alternate adolescence you didn't actually live? When chopping wood to make an axe handle, you don't have to look far to find the pattern: there's one on page 73 of the catalog. Thank goodness for identity theft; otherwise, our markets wouldn't keep expanding.

Octopuses React to Predator and Prey on TV. Goliath, the "Giant" Cat. Since everything that is not me is nature, I always speak in my outside voice. Toddler and Cat's Funny Wrestling Match. She was a "celebrity farmer." They were poor, so I knew they wouldn't find a fake rat as funny as a real one. India to Weaponize World's Hottest Chili.

So I figured, why not put body heat to work *for me*? I eye-droppered some water into the stream and said, "I've invented perpetual motion." I couldn't believe it: she was paying attention, and she wasn't even a sociologist. I didn't punch him. I am mute and my hand has Tourette's syndrome. My powers frighten even me: I didn't expect to see him there, so I didn't see him, and it turns out *he wasn't there*.

I stood in the rain of light and got wet. I stood in the light rain and dried off. The blueberry was so fresh it mooed when my fork touched it. The program focused on three amazing people "whose brains have taken over their bodies." The atmosphere is my anti-oxidant.

I knew enough to realize it was one of the world's most dangerous stuffed animals. The difference between "it remains" and "its remains" remained there for all to see. At least the special tang in the gas station's fried chicken is unleaded.

The person with the most power grades the essays on "social structures." They said their smiles were "surfaces;" we thought they were "surface effects." Here at Oil Pollution Control, we like to say, "birds of a feather stick together." He said, *But who'll forgive me if I have not said / What path you make me tread?* and I said I will, so, see, everything's better.

The more static the chart, the more undiluted the motion it represents. We finally contacted the aliens, but our methods of communication acted as white noise on each other's nervous systems, so both groups fell asleep.

There's always something extra in light. When my grandfather said I was in his light, he meant I was between him and the TV.

Mark Cunningham received an MFA from the University of Virginia, and he lives now in central Missouri. If time were flexible and he could do whatever he wanted to, he'd be a Paleolithic cave artist. In particular, he would like to sculpt the two clay bison at the end of Le Tuc D'Audoubert. Since that seems unlikely to happen, or to have happened, he's taken to watching rugby on TV. He's also written three books—*80 Beetles*, *Body Language*, and *71 Leaves*—and, now, *specimens*, a book he thinks is, you know, pretty OK.

Made in the USA
Monee, IL
07 July 2026